A CONTEMPLATIVE LIFE

A CONTEMPLATIVE LIFE

LYNN CRONIN GEER

Onion River Press
89 Church Street
Burlington, VT 05401
info@onionriverpress.com
www.onionriverpress.com

ISBN: 978-1-957184-91-3
Library of Congress Control Number: 2024922939

Contents

Overcome with the Love of God, filled with His presence I cannot believe I ever ran from such loveliness, that I tried to escape this all-encompassing joy. I believe I suffered but I cannot remember it. I am sure I was alone, but all that seems unreal. I must have felt fear, but now there is only faith. I breathe forth every breath with humility.

LCG

Preface

Silence is a doorway to the divine, a kind of stargate that first ephemerally then continuously brings the seeker to the infinite. This path is attractive as a way of life to only a few. Although many active souls enjoy spiritual quiet, they do not pursue the vast emptiness of silence. It is in silence that God speaks to the contemplative, showing Himself like a vortex that sends souls spinning to the Void. The feeling of being drawn into the One, lost in the divine metaphor, is the end of silence. After the overpowering loneliness, after the emotional desert, after the sea of doubt, there are the moments of perfect silence when God speaks to the contemplative and bestows upon him the garment of eternal Love. For this the contemplative will endure anything.

Do you sense that there is something missing in your life?

This book is for people who already know that God or the One is in their lives.

From the time I was small I was called to God alone. I could never get enough of church or prayer. This was simply when I was the happiest. I was sad when I had to stop praying, unhappy when a service ended. Even if I did not like the sermon, I could not wait till communion. Now many years later I am still the same, still moved to tears of joy by the presence of God. However, I was afraid to put everything aside for God. I wanted to be normal. No matter how I struggled against it, however, God continually called to me. The harder I worked to have what I considered a normal life, the more God asked me to join Him in prayer. The contemplative is made to listen to God and to know Him intimately. It is not that the contemplative is designed for a higher mode of existence, or set above the rest of humanity, but instead is attracted to a life of prayer, silence and separateness. The contemplative knows this with every fiber of his being and is drawn to the One above all else. Though often tempted by worldly things, the contemplative sometimes feels he is cheating God by giving in to his own desires. The world is immediate but the One is hidden; the world is easy but the One is difficult; the world satisfies the appetites but the One calls the contemplative to a life of solitude.

God waits for the contemplative no matter how far he travels from the straight path first offered. When he finally returns to the One, ragged and scarred from the journey, God welcomes him home with the dizzying heat of His boundless hospitality. I believed that God would be angry with me, not only because I had ignored His initial invitation, but also because I had justified my decision. However, God is the fountainhead of mercy, not like the capricious gods of old. As the monks of the Weston Priory sing: "Come back to me with all your heart. Don't let fear keep us apart. Long have I waited for your coming home to me and living deeply our new life." They affirm what many contemplatives know through experience, that God is ever patient with those He has called to Himself.

Exordium

In the 13th century, Aquinas wrote that there are two ways to live: active and contemplative. He discussed the separateness of the active and contemplative lives. According to his view, the active person spends his time living in the obvious world, concerning himself with day-to-day matters, friends, family, work, play and even prayer. Theirs is the temporal life. For the contemplative, however, life is a quest where the One is sought above all else. Now the great monasteries of the past are nearly empty. The stalls and chanceries, once spiritual powerhouses, are dusty monuments to art, scholarly pursuits or curiosities for tourists. Reduced to a smaller number of men and women who perhaps have greater courage than their brothers and sisters of the past, contemplative monks and sisters function as emblems of love, integrity, justice and peace for those who live in the world. They lead lives of great value, seeking God and working for Him in the vineyard of the 21st century. Now the line between the active and contemplative life has blurred, and most called to prayer live among us working out their vocation far from the bells of the cloister. For these courageous men and women, like their companions, God and prayer are central to each action, so that people they meet are touched with the glory and the healing grace of the One who gave them breath. Their mission is to save souls through prayer so that God's love will be made manifest on earth, completing a circle of love begun by the Creator, glorified in all His persons, signified by those set apart devoted only to Him, and continued in the worldly battlefield. Each person has within him the seeds of both the active and contemplative spirit, although those drawn to worldly things often sublimate their desire for the eternal in the quest for lives of comfort. However, the more actively oriented can and should develop the contemplative part of their persona, allowing for spiritual experience and an increase of faith rather than mere religious practice. If God is sought, He will not remain hidden, regardless of an individual's religious affiliation. This is a book of the spirit rather than one of a particular religious group Although as a Western person I am a Christian, God has many names, and the contemplative soul is drawn to Him, not His name. Those called to God above all else know this in the depth of their being, and it is for them, my brothers and sisters, that I have written what follows, but others who long for a more intimate relationship with God and moments of perfect joy may find a path in these pages.

Long before I understood what the word meant, I naively told my mentor that I planned to write a book to help contemplatives live in the world. That was before the letters to the Carmelites, the marriage, death, divorce, and the ensuing despair. That was before my phoenix rose from the ashes of pain and delivered me to the mountain of joy. So before I could write the book, I needed to live the life. For me, suffering was necessary to an understanding of the cosmic mysteries and the gift I had been given. For as long as I can remember, I was called to be one apart. I was an only child. I used to make tents from blankets and place them near our flower gardens, sometimes by the hollyhocks, sometimes by the peonies. I think my mother worried about me because she thought I should be roller-skating or playing in the swing. I just sat there with my books reading or pretending to read. Actually, I enjoyed not reading. The sounds and smells of the garden come back to me as clearly as if only a moment has passed. I see the pale blue world I created from inside my tent and remember the peace and happiness that kept me free of the outside world. The bees and dragonflies hummed to the silent songs of the garden. When I sat near the goldfish pond, I imagined the noises the tails of the fish made as they moved in the clear water. This is when I began to listen. I learned I could listen best alone, and although I was not sure what or who I was listening to, I knew that this was magical, a wonderful present.

When I went to school, every Monday there was religious release time. I walked behind the bigger kids to St. Anthony's Church. In the dark basement we were taught our catechism. The nuns who taught us scared me, but each week I would slip through the swinging doors into the church itself. I remember thinking that God was talking to me amid the statues and the marble, that behind the crosses and frescoes of the saints, God spoke to me through the stones. The nuns would tell us to hurry along, but I did not pay attention. That was the beginning of my contemplative life. Nothing was better than the divine conversation.

The negative words and actions of others rise up like soldiers in a video game, ready to kill the hero. They are so quick and so arresting that they take up the whole screen, easily overwhelming anyone in their path. They seem to require all the attention because they are so threatening. They bear their problems and thrust them forward like weapons demanding to be reckoned with. Contemplatives living in the world are often distracted by these forces, forgetting that they are to love their neighbor as themselves, not the other way around. Nothing that damages the spirit should be sought, for the Lord has chosen contemplatives to share His silence and know Him intimately.

The contemplative life can sometimes lead to disillusionment. I have given myself to a God I cannot see, to a system of belief I can not physically prove, to a life which outwardly makes little sense. I have set goals that my friends and family question, and often cause rebuke. I have little to show that I have walked upon this planet or have achieved any kind of worldly success. Sometimes, I cannot even explain my life to myself. I am tempted by a world that runs on money and pleasure, where people move ahead in discernible increments and are rewarded for their trouble. I see others enjoying the closeness of relationships, standing in line together at the supermarket, smiling in anticipation of a shared meal, while I am alone. In these times,

God withdraws Himself from me, leaving me in the barrenness of His desert. Reason fails, and logic falls away. I remind myself that my feelings, however tortuous, are creations of my own ego, designed by me to rise against my next transformation.

I cling, Lord, to your love remembered, to your promises stronger than death. I beg for the grace to assuage my doubts and the courage to persevere when you hide your face from me. I prostrate myself before you, calling out for mercy from this gift of wilderness.

THE PATH

Bob Lax has written, what if you wish to paint big flowers, but the rules of art say to paint only straight lines? Then you should paint big flowers, big flowers, big flowers until they become straight lines, straight lines, straight lines. So it is with the problem of the One and the many. Active people find pleasure in the many forms in nature, seeing them as separate from themselves. They struggle to learn to understand, to delve deeply, to study difference, to compare and contrast. They experiment and record their data. They write articles for journals to explain their findings and the meanings of their work. As contemplatives observe the world and the people who inhabit it in silence, they begin to narrow the gap between themselves and the people who inhabit it, slowly awakening to the idea that each form is really a repetition of the One, or another view of the eternal prism. The hope for active people is that they continue to peruse the world of the many till they see only the One. The contemplative knows this instinctually, realizing it fully in silence, which cleanses the mind and heart, uniting him to the single object of his desire. This is why the life of the contemplative is so maligned, for if the contemplative is right, then it may seem that most of what active persons live for is incorrect, or worse than that, maybe a lie.

I tell my students to find their path, and to stay on it. This is the great secret of life for the active and contemplative person. I have had many active souls tell me that they did not know what or where their path was, and I just tell them that their path is before them. I have been accused of giving out few details. Yet as the years have gone on, they write me letters, call me, send me emails. They know that I didn't know anything about their particular future, but I did know that they should search for what they wanted to do, even if the search took some strange turns. Inside, each of them knew all along what their path was, what would make them happy, what people would add to their lives and what relationships would detract from it. All they had to do was remain honest with themselves. Now as they reach middle age and beyond, some have never found what they wanted, but they have stayed on the path anyway because it was the truest thing they could do. For the contemplatives I have taught, however, the path has been more difficult, leading many to the panoply of misery the world is happy to provide. This is because there are so few ways for the contemplative to fulfill his obligation and heed his call to God and live joyously in the world because the contemplative life is both obscure and esoteric.

It is difficult to describe a life whose goal is simply to know the heart of God, to experience the One of creation. This is not listed on anyone's list of possible careers for high school graduates. The contemplative vocation is not always understandable to those called to the active life. A life of solitude and silence may be acceptable if one is a poet or philosopher but seems bizarre if there are no accomplishments to balance this peculiar choice of path. The contemplative who seeks God first may even be misunderstood and mistrusted by church officials and those dedicated to expression of faith, who see good works teaching of holy books as being the best way to live a religiously oriented life. Therefore, the contemplative may feel abandoned by those he has sworn to love. The world is produced and directed by active people. Giving each other the starring roles, they lead corporations, administer educational institutions, promulgate laws, manage bureaucracies and work for success. They even influence entertainment, sports and religion. They set goals, reading self-help books to enhance their communication skills. They are circumspect, carefully recording schedules and meetings in day planners so that they can move up the ladder to recognition and lucre. These are the people that make things happen, the organizers and makers of modern society. They are good men and women who work, play, and measure themselves against established criterion. As leaders of the new order, they force members of society to adhere to their rules and follow their regulations. They remain busy, developing habits that will further their progress. It is not easy for them to understand those who do not really want to do anything special but wish only to be receptacles for God's love or disappear into nothingness.

Therefore contemplatives often feel that they are ineffective because they do not measure up to the exacting standards the active world has set down for them. They sometimes doubt their own worth and question the value of a life which means so little by the standards of active men and women. It is no wonder then that many contemplatives languish in indecision, finding it hard to believe that God has chosen them to live solely for Him. They remain in the doorway, unwilling to accept the contemplative life. This is foolish, for in truth they are running away from their true selves, the singular purpose for which they were born. Their indecision is a sign of spiritual weakness and diminished hope, becoming a trap that bars them from the love the One is always ready to shower upon them.

The One is the best of Communicators. He has spoken to man from the ancient philosophers, from Hesiod's creation and Heraclitus' river of change, and from the prophets of the Old Testament: from Moses and Leviticus. He has spoken from the writers of the East: from Chuang Tzu, and from Buddha and his followers, from Mohammed and the writers of the Koran. He has called to us from the pages of the New Testament, from Mark, John, Paul, and the others, and from the words of his very Son. He has even exhorted us from the souls of poets and writers, who follow His divine inspiration. When this was not enough, He has shown man His face in nature, in the blooming of trees and the falling of petals, in the smell of juniper and magnolia, in the fierceness of blizzards and the might of mountains, in the gentle rain and the faint heartbeat of animals. The One tries with such sweet patience to reach His creatures with faith, hope and love. The world needs the contemplative to be His envoy, to provide the cosmic earphones and corrective lenses. The contemplative is the humble messenger, whose life of prayer and solitude raises the head of man that he might not sleep but see and hear.

The One calls the weak and the foolish, the cowardly and the prideful, those bent on revenge or addicted to their own desires. He calls them until they surrender even unto death. Then He fashions them anew in the garments of poverty, in the sandals of obedience. He feeds them the bread of His wilderness until they want no meat. He offers them the wine of His blood until they no longer thirst. He wraps them in the cloak of solitude until they long for His silence. They become the purified heart of His mystical body, beating in time with His universe, saving souls through prayer and their own blessed redemption. The One has planned this from the beginning, waiting until just the right moment in time for their transformation, offering them the grace to live their new life.

SIMPLICITY

In all things be a beginner, for as the ancients say, fortune smiles on our first effort. Do not be so wise that wisdom itself becomes a goal, for wisdom can be the burden of the pedant and causes his shuffling step. Be open to the world of possibilities, for as a beginner there is no pressure to succeed, little opportunity for failure. Be full of enthusiasm, hope and the promise of what is to come. Stay observant, taking in each new image as though it were a wondrous gift, not hampered by looking for what is expected. Follow directions with a buoyant heart and be willing to practice what is learned. Approach each new task with childlike curiosity and reverence, embracing the unknown, because for the beginner, even what is difficult seems easy. The beginner is ready for God to enter, unafraid of His power, unaffected by the swells of His infinite sea.

What is there to do when God seems far away and His words become hollow anthems, impractical, even meaningless? Then the contemplative must simply wait, knowing that somehow, he had left God behind, not the other way around. I often feel myself moving away from God, involving myself too much in daily activities, to such a degree that I forget my true purpose. I see my duties as an end in themselves and lose my way, drifting from my path. Then only the active world is real, and prayer becomes first perfunctory and finally mere duty. Thus I often bring about my own suffering and then blame God for abandoning me. Only when I retreat to solitude and diligently wait for inner silence does God return, ever merciful in spite of my foolishness.

It is in nature that complexities become simple. There is a small lake in upstate New York called Good Luck Lake. Deep in the Adirondacks, it is permeated with the scent of pine and hemlock, a Zen lake of both finite and infinite proportions. It is too small for big boats with noisy engines, but for canoes with wooden paddles that slip through the water. I seldom caught any fish there and the mosquitoes have their way with visitors, yet the lake is a spot of perfect harmony, where fish jump just beyond the reach of the line and red-tailed hawks fly close to the surface in indolent spirals. This is the perfect blending of energy and lassitude, where waterbugs slide close to the shore, where the bullfrogs wait, where the living hum and the dead rest in the loam. There is serenity of water and the pain of insect bites, where the fish die so that we may eat. This is the table of the Lord, where we are called to supper.

Only when life is lived authentically is it lived fully. A life that denies the true self brings only temporary happiness, for it is based on pretense. God calls us to joy, showing us in a myriad of ways what leads to fulfillment, asking us to listen and follow the path best suited to our particular psyche. What is authentic feels right, and deep in our hearts we know it. If we are called to a life of prayer, we are most joyful when we are at prayer, even if it is easier to live in a more prosaic fashion. Therefore it is important to reflect, to examine the heart, to respond to God within us, to be real to others and ourselves. This is the central responsibility of each person, achieving authenticity, no matter what the cost.

One of my students spoke in his church about the love of God, silencing his listeners, reminding them that the love of God was stronger than their individual wills, greater than they could ever imagine. He knew from their rapt attention that his audience understood that God had spoken through him. God loves us completely, showering us each day with love beyond measure. Never considering our worthiness, our good deeds or our bad actions, God pours love upon us indiscriminately, waiting patiently for the crystal moment of our recognition. It is not the resurrection that is so unbelievable; that God should die and rise again is part of both ancient and modern faith systems. That God should love us in our frailty and ambiguity, and that He should love us unconditionally beyond our own understanding of love, is the great mystery of creation. Whether I am angry or calm, cling to the past or act with courage, God is not concerned. His love is constant and real. Saints understand the love of God, basking in it. They know God in His love and are forged in its fire until they are holy. They are not so much ready to die for the love of God but rather to live for it. This is because they have recognized the wonder of God's love and allowed themselves, through grace, to be a part of it. Thus they live in the real world while mere believers do not.

When Jeremiah was told he was to be a prophet he objected. He knew that if he told the Israelites that Jerusalem would be destroyed, that the gap between the rich and poor was not Godly, he would in turn be rejected by his own people. Yet he answered God's call, "Before you were born, I consecrated you, and appointed you my prophet." So, Jeremiah preached for 40 years, but men did not heed him. In 587, Jerusalem was sacked, the temple ruined, and the rulers were killed. For his decades of trouble, Jeremiah was taken hostage and probably murdered. Yet he did not turn away; he followed his difficult path, assenting to the commands of God. Like Jeremiah, I too am a bearer of God's light and wisdom. Let me accept His will beyond my own objections and change the corner of the world He has given me to change.

Now there are new prophets for this new age. At the same time some TV shows lure audiences with the possibility of seven figure rewards if they will only: lie or be cruel, or eliminate the best people or fight fears by letting rats bite them, new prophets are emerging. They are the voices of God making Himself heard in a society moved forward by greed. They respond to a call to prayer in action, bringing churches together for community service, healing young and old with love and compassion, bringing hope to the poor and the spiritually needy. They are aided not only by religious leaders by also by those in the new temples of media who use money and power for the betterment of mankind and glory of God. These are the blest few who serve the many at the banquet of love. The power behind Oprah, Amazon.com, Habitat for Humanity and the rest is not money but prayer, driving benefactors to give of their wealth so that the less fortunate may receive. Though now the great spiritual citadels of the Middle Ages have become tourist attractions, the psalms chorused by hundred now chanted by a few, the prayer itself continues. In each church and synagogue, mosque, and temple there are a small number whose prayers send continual petition, praise and thanksgiving to the God of creation and His spirit among us. Sometimes in small groups, sometimes alone, they carry on the work of the ages, fulfilling the divine commandment, reestablishing moment by moment a holy internet, born in suffering, transformed by love. Like those who build and heal, they also serve, strengthening the work of God through the purity of prayer. Yet they often remain in secret, an army armed with divine truth and love, battling the evil of the world, which is ever ready to obliterate them and their message. Like the prophets of old they are pursued by enemies, who attack them on every side, who try to destroy what Merton calls the Hidden Ground of Love. Even people within their own religious community may misunderstand their vocation to prayer and power of prayer alone, encouraging them to preach God's word to others. Fortunately for the world, a great number persist, and the lifeline of prayer is kept in place. "Pray always; pray always; pray always"; the modern psalmist lifts up his heart so that the love of God may grow in the world claiming souls for Him.

What is bad for us casts us into unnecessary suffering and turmoil; what is good for us produces internal harmony and peace. This is inherently simple, but not many remember this in the flow of interactive life. When I am wrestling with a difficult problem, I know, deep in my heart, what to do. I just don't want to accept what should be done. Instead I create a myriad of solutions so I won't have to do what I know to be the best thing for me. This is an enigma of the human condition. Why do I choose peril and pain? Do I not trust God to give me as much as I can handle? In the not-too-distant future people may be taped from the moment of birth until they die. Disease will be conquered, and death will occur only when the human machine finally runs out of options. Perhaps then the movie of life will be, as had been suggested, shown to me. Will I, like some football coach, pace on the sideline of my life, saying, "Oh, shucks," as I watch myself miss play after play, sabotaging my own touchdowns? This is why I pray and live my life as best I can, so that does not happen.

Lord, let me choose what is best for me in the light of Your wisdom. Grant me peace.

LONGING

In a series of holiday greetings, Thomas Merton wrote, "God bless all the women who can not find a thing to wear on the racks at Bergdorf Goodman." No material goods, no human interaction, no drug is a substitute for the Love of God. Throughout my life I have been filled with inexplicable longing. The feeling accompanied an ache in the back of my throat that would not go away, that awakened with me in the morning, lessened with the business of the day, and haunted my nights. I wondered what I had done wrong, why nothing satisfied me, why no one loved me enough. In college, after a late-night party, I sometimes wept. There was a priest there that said Mass in a tiny chapel. Only five or six people ever attended, the rest perhaps preferring a larger community or a liturgy with music. Father Gulley's Mass was filled with what I recognize now to be contemplative prayer. Sometimes I rushed there like an escape. There I no longer felt like a dervish, trying madly to dine on the worldly banquet. There with that reverent spirit I was at least momentarily content. Father Gulley contended that we came to his Mass because it was, as he said, "a fifteen-minute special." This was a great joke between us, because we all knew we were there to meet God in silence.

Longing is not dissatisfaction; it is instead a feeling that there is some great purpose that is somehow being missed. It is the one thing that the contemplative cannot deny. This is the divine call that begs the contemplative to enter into the One for his own good. It is God's sign that the contemplative belongs to Him and no one else. Longing defies logic. It is not congruent with the habits of what is considered normal society. In the 4th century, the Desert Fathers went off into the wilds of North Africa. No matter how far into the wilderness they went, students followed them. Even they could not entirely shed the bonds of everyday life. So too Buddha left the world until he was shown under the Bohdi tree that he was a teacher of men. Surrender is the cure for longing, daily, even hourly surrender to the One who created the contemplative in Love to be His servant. This is the great contemplative struggle, for just as the Desert Fathers fled their disciples and Siddartha was reluctant to tread the middle way, so too the contemplative may fight against the will of God until he accepts the sweetness of surrender.

Free will gives the contemplative the idea that he can do whatever he likes, but in a way, it is a grand illusion. I had a great desire to be like other people, so I made a life plan and stuck to it. I did not want to be different. I wanted a husband, an ordinary life. I was afraid to give my heart to a voice in my head, to give up everything other people understood to lead a life that filled me with fear. I believed I could assuage my longing with my will and intellect. Longing will not be subdued, will not give into replacement therapy. Longing is a recognition that the soul chosen for a specific purpose is separate from God. Longing chases down the soul until it finally falls down and submits to God's act of love.

At one point the One becomes the Beloved, asking detachment from worldly things. One by one all else falls away. The things so important initially begin to fade and God alone takes center stage. It is hard to remember basic goals or even a "to do" list. With detachment comes acceptance, then wonder, that God would choose the individual as a receptacle for His gifts. God becomes the director, and all actions follow His divine plan. Fortunately, longing is never slaked. The soul enters a cycle where again and again there is loneliness, emptiness and doubt, a place where these challenges are conquered by the act of surrender, where daily prayer and compassion for fellow men combines with work to bring joy. Therefore, periods of darkness bring light, loneliness mutuality, emptiness fullness of spirit, and doubt confidence.

Longing sends the contemplative on a spiritual journey, past the towns and cities, far from the highways and the well-trod paths until he enters the One, who has been knocking on the doorway to his heart all along, asking, sometimes demanding entrance. This is a beautiful dichotomy, that what is within is longed for, that what is hidden lies patent, that what seems obscure is truly clear. Finally, the contemplative finds the place his feet have been seeking on the summit of mystical delight, in splendor of luminous darkness. The transience and momentary triumph of earthly union is little in comparison to the love God showers on those He has marked with His seal.

As the Lord is one in us may we be one in Him
As we surrender to Him
And pass into the sea of unknowing
We reappear in a radiant edition of our former selves
A musical phrase of wondrous harmony
On the mountain of light
Where God needs but to whisper

PAIN

P ain is a necessity if longing is to intensify. Therefore God works at the contemplative as though He were husking an ear of corn, taking from him the things of the world that stand in the way of his longing for God. The more the contemplative ties himself to possessions, career or relationships that do not have their center in Him, the more God relentlessly takes away what will ultimately damage his child's ability to receive His love. The contemplative who persists in his own stubbornness will bring upon himself untold pain and suffering. This is the great difference between the active and contemplative soul. Each is different in a fundamental way. The active person moves along an easily understood path, where one task connects with the next, where success is measured in the adherence to a set of rules, in good works done. The active person has gratitude for the life of Christ and the salvation His humanness has brought. He works and prays, raising his eyes to the One who gave him life. The contemplative lets God take him in an act of voluntary surrender. If he lives in the world he must submit to the Word, reluctant as he is to divinity. This is a world where events only connect in retrospect when the lesson taught by the Beloved is to some measure understood. Pain is corrective, a necessity for progress, a spiritual advisor for those who desire purity of heart.

When Christ called out, "Abba, Abba," He cried for all of us, when we ask, "Why have You forsaken me?" He knew that He was dying for those who would build His churches, follow His precepts, honor His covenants, that He was dying that they might live on forever in Him. Just as He had to die for the active souls who would people

His churches, He suffered intense loneliness, despair, and dread for those who had been called to share the mystery of spiritual death and wrenching surrender. Active souls went on to preach His Word, to teach the message of the Gospels. They gathered together, invented rituals and preserved His promises. Contemplatives followed Him into the desert, where like Him they were stripped of their garments and made ready for sacrifice. Like Him they did so alone. They paid little attention to the promise of eternal life. Instead, they became attentive to each moment, each breath. It is their job to carry on His words, "Abba, Abba, why have you forsaken me?" It is their duty to live out the contemplative vocation as did Christ and His messengers.

GRATITUDE

When I was in the seventh grade, I was in a play in which a boy (who later became a doctor) acted the part of an ailing world. The plot—such as it was—hinged on those trying to cure the earth's malady. I offered "great works of literature, philosophy, and sculptured masterpieces" in my mother's mouton lamb jacket. My treatment, of course, was unsuccessful. It was only when an innocent child gave faith, hope and love that the world revived and became well. Ironically, I spent many years pursuing the very gifts that failed to help the earth. Beautifully written books, reason and art provided me with a measure of happiness, but they did not bring me joy. Instead they often left me empty and hollow. Although the works contained unity, harmony and brilliance, they were only tools I used to feed my own ego. Perhaps the artists and philosophers had seen God in what they created, but I saw only my own ability to marshal knowledge and surpass those in my way. Now life is much simpler. I seek to know God better in whatever way He presents himself to me. I have only to look, and God is there.

Gratitude is a gift of the spirit, making what has been dreaded a treasure, because it proceeds from the One. It is not only for gifts received that gratitude is appropriate but also for requests withheld. Rejection teaches a preference for God's love above all and is of itself a great blessing. It places the individual at the mercy of his Father who will give him greater love than mankind can offer. It is through rejection that the contemplative can come closer to the One that calls him and be grateful for even the little things that make his life rich.

Rejection clears the vision so that warm food, cool drink and even noisy woodpeckers become the sanctified gifts the One has prepared for those who know Him. Gratitude makes ordinary life and extraordinary pleasure, heightening awareness, charging each moment with wonder.

When God calls the contemplative to the desert, he becomes confronted with his own nothingness and the meaninglessness of his actions. Prayers of gratitude can guide him out of the dark emptiness and bring him once more into the lush hillsides of hope. When the contemplative cries out to God for mercy, begs Him for help and thanks Him for all that he has given up, all that he has become, he takes up his cross of acceptance and willingly goes forward without regret. Gratitude opens the heart to the mercy of God, just as thanklessness closes it tight like a fist, stopping the self-inflicted suffering that some unwisely call sacrifice. It is in gratitude that hope is realized, and the brightness of God first thought to be darkness is seen as overwhelming light.

The contemplative like other men tries to find God's will for him. Actually God does give signs all the time. Man refuses to notice. He keeps doing the same thing over and over again, and when each time the result is negative, he merely tries again, refusing to believe that any sign has been given, believing instead that he should try again with greater determination, even when the results of his efforts make him miserable. The simple truth is that man is doing God's will every moment he lives in accordance with what he knows to be right, not according to what he wants, but according to what he believes is the right thing for him. God may not tell his creature what kind of sandwich to get from the delicatessen, but He will show him his path.

We are the vessels of the One, holding the bread and wine of spiritual life. It is for us to be the bearers of food and drink, to be filled and to be broken, to be repaired, filled, and broken again. We are part of a heritage of hidden souls, reaching back to that first consecration, a silent legacy of contempla-

tive prayer. We do this in remembrance of Him. As the One uses us, we are humbled, lower than the servant, we are mere dispensers of His chrism that gives courage to those crying out for mercy. We are nothing in ourselves and everything in Him. When we are empty, He fills us. When we are cracked and broken, His touch makes us new. When we are cast aside, He alone remembers us. We hold the water that washes the feet of his disciples, and we delight in the Lord for the humility we gratefully receive. Praise God our Steward and Everlasting Lord. Praise His wondrous hospitality welcoming us to the ministry of prayer.

SILENCE AND SOLITUDE

According to the Myers-Briggs Test, about 40% of the subjects get their energy from being alone. Of these, about 1/5 prefer silence to any sound, even music. Silence is a healing balm, a powerful force, a source of God's infinite grace. It is in silence that the contemplative can rest from the noise of the world, find refuge from the snares of human contact. Silence allows the contemplative to empty his mind, thus freeing himself from his self-appointed tasks, and detaching himself from those concerns, no matter how "good" they may be in themselves, that keep him from being devoured by God. It is in silence that the contemplative fulfills his purpose, to become a person of prayer, a soul who belongs to God alone. Without silence there can be no deep state of prayer, no complete openness to God's Word, no surrender to God's will. For a contemplative living in the world silence is a great challenge. It is difficult to find the time or even the place to be silent. Phones ring, people drop by, music from next door blares loudly. Without silence the contemplative spirit will wither and face. He will become hollow and desolate, unless there is silence in his life.

Solitude is the proper companion of silence. The Anchoresses of the Desert who, like their male counterparts, entered the vast emptiness of North Africa, did not write very much about their experiences, but praised solitude as the rock of their prayer and meditation. Surprisingly, the Desert Fathers were quite vocal for all their praise of solitude in the contemplative life, but their warnings about value of the solitary experience have been vital guides for the brother and sisters who have followed them. When the contemplative is alone, set apart from the company of others he is available to God. It is as though a veil falls over him, sheltering him in the Cloud of Unknowing. In solitude God can enter the contemplative soul and reveal the mystery of His Love. However, solitude leaves the contemplative vulnerable, open to both the wounds and the delights of Love. Here again is the dichotomy the contemplative faces on a daily basis: the union of suffering and joy, of loneliness and bliss, of hope and despair. This is his great struggle.

The more I watch television and listen to radio, the more I am convinced that there are many contemplatives who do not know who they are, and therefore wander through life listening to advice that may be great for active people but simply does not suit the contemplative life. Therefore, the tools suggested to repair the active souls wounded by the world are not often appropriate for the contemplative who is suffering. Although human relationships are important, they exist only peripherally to the contemplative's relationship with the One, who wishes to be first in all things. When the monks at Weston pray "for our absent brothers and sisters", I always think of those men and women lost in a sea of possessions and burdened with other people's dreams.

While I worked for a major corporation, I was amazed at how effectively the corporate mind invaded every aspect of my life. I remember the beautiful surroundings, the soundless escalators and the verdant greenery. In the narrow passages and wide corridors there was an unyielding silence and in the cubicles real solitude. Glass pillars rose skyward while good people labored mindful of their every move. Success was visualized, dedicated work was praised and rewarded. Everywhere there were dutiful footsteps, heads inclined to corporate trust. This is the new monasticism, built by men who understand the great edifices and voracious spirit of Pericles, who in praise of lucre gather hearts and minds together, binding them through beneficial work to their creed. Within these walls many contemplatives satisfy their need to do good in silence and solitude and to forget their call to prayer rather than stock options.

Leo Lionni's *Frederick* at first seems to be merely an entertaining children's book. It tells the story of a little mouse who, when all the other mice were getting ready for winter, was quietly reflective. When they asked him why he wasn't working, he contended that he too was gathering valuable supplies. When winter came, at first the mice enjoyed the oats and corn they had gathered, but when it was gone they huddled together waiting for death. Remembering Frederick's promises, they asked him for his store of goods. He not only made them feel warmth and hope but helped them believe in a kind of mice-god as well. Frederick was a contemplative mouse, realizing that his best supplies were not derived from regular labor but rather from what he learned in silence. He was able to translate this to give hope and trust to his brothers and sisters. The book speaks to the value of the poets among us but, on a deeper level, to those whose work it is to pray for the rest, even if their prayers are silent and even if only God hears them. Contemplatives elevate the work of active men and women, sanctifying mundane lives by imbuing them with God's Love. They transmit divine energy and call down blessings upon those who work in the darkness of the human spirit. They give strength to those who labor for the poor, bereft and the disenfranchised. They open the hearts of those who yearn to know God, and those who are like themselves but live in fear of their vocation.

Although it is true that the contemplative benefits from prayer in common with other members of a congregation and adds a positive force to any group gathered for prayer, it is good to remember that the contemplative is first of all called to solitude. This is the way God shows Himself to His child, filling him with boundless Grace. It is through intimate and Divine sharing that God brands the contemplative with the fire of His Infinite Love, so that he can fill the empty vessels of the poor in spirit. When the contemplative prays with others, just as when he works actively his spirit is used by those near him who need what he seems to have in abundance. Thus time alone with God is necessary if the contemplative is going to replenish his spiritual supplies and continue to be a wellspring of love and hope for others. The danger is that the contemplative will allow himself to be drained of God's love and to be cast adrift, bereft, alone and empty. I no longer let this happen, I repair myself, spending time alone with God in silence and solitude. For many years I emptied my cup, until I was nearly dead from giving to others what only belonged to God. I took pity on myself for my pain, mistakenly thinking that God wanted a martyr when all he asked for was a faithful servant. I thought God loved me because of my gifts, when all he expected was a humble and quiet "Yes."

PRAYER

Prayer is the center of the contemplative life, both consecrating and elevating action. Through a constant flow of prayer the contemplative offers his life again and again to God, asking God to walk with him as he completes the smallest of tasks. This is the process that the Buddhists call mindfulness, where each step, each seemingly insignificant movement, each breath taken is given total attention. Therefore nothing is unimportant, so that the individual focuses on those things he has not noticed before in his daily routine. This is a way to hold what the Zen monks call a beginner's mind, seeing each moment with new eyes. Thus, in prayer the contemplative stays ever alert and awake, keeping the words spoken often, new, keeping his mind and heart ready like a child for God's messages. If prayer becomes humdrum, the contemplative has lost his purpose. He cannot fall back on his last raise or great review at the office. Therefore, he must pray always with a beginner's mind, staying in touch with the divine conversation.

The goal of post-reformation Christianity is a personal relationship with Jesus Christ as a brother and Savior, in which believers break down the barriers between themselves and Him who they worship. The contemplative moves beyond this, knowing that like the three brothers of the Old Testament who were cast into the fiery furnace, the flames of Divine Love will not burn him, because he will become part of the flames themselves. He becomes One with the fire by means of contemplative prayer. The method is like that of the Zen monks, the Hindu yogis, the Moslem holy men, who direct their lives to God in an attempt to know Him intimately. They develop habits of silent prayer, training their minds, hearts and bodies to respond to the rigorous discipline such prayer demands. When prayer is honest and couched in humility, the contemplative moves forward on his path; when prayer if perfunctory and self-serving, it is of no use to anyone, even the person at prayer. This is a demanding course that requires a devotion to solitude. As Merton reminds us using the words of St. Bernard: "Sit alone, have nothing in common with the crowd, nothing with the multitude of others ... Holy soul, remain alone and keep yourself for Him alone out of all others." It is difficult to remain "out of the swing of the sea" for contemplatives who live in the world. There is always the tearing of the spirit, whether to work or to pray, whether to help others or to meditate on the Lord, whether to satisfy everyday desires or to shut out all else but the desire for God. As the contemplative matures these concerns disappear and all actions become the same. Prayer hones the soul, smoothing, correcting, shaping it until it is a perfect arrow point to pierce the heart of the Beloved.

Overcome with the Love of God, filled with His presence I cannot believe I ever ran from such loveliness, that I tried to escape this all-encompassing joy. I believe I suffered but I cannot remember it. I am sure I was alone, but all that seems unreal. I must have felt fear, but now there is only faith. I breathe forth every breath with humility and trust, remembering only these days, these nights.

As the Lord is One in us may we be One in Him.

DARKNESS

Darkness is both enemy and beloved. In darkness there is dread that God will see the contemplative in all his nakedness and steal away even the empty shell of his familiar being. In the darkness there is the terror of the unknown, the fear that there will be nothing left after the One destroys the ego, that an unrecognizable image will stare back from the contemplative's mirror. The contemplative may lose his way in a labyrinth of fear, unable to navigate the darkness because his path demands maturity not cosmic dramatics, suffering not the pretense of suffering.

The contemplative is often reluctant to bear the weight of the rigors his life demands. He is deeply afraid that the new life of the spirit will be overwhelmingly difficult without informal human interaction, that the promise offered will be without warmth and laughter. Most of all, the contemplative is afraid of being alone in the darkness, misunderstood by his friends and family, separated from human love, which is pleasant and comfortable. This confrontation with fear is a necessary part of this path. Here many turn away and build a life blending the contemplative with the active. Only a few risk everything known to grope through the darkness to light, to enter into the One and swell beneath its blinding beams. For this traveler darkness is the beloved who comes in the night, covering the initiate with his wings, taking even his breath, till he dies to himself and is restored to the brilliance from which he came.

The contemplative often grieves when torn from prayer, like a child ordered from leisure to do his chores. He knows that his true work is to communicate with God in the silence of prayer and meditation, talking to God and listening to Him. Therefore, in the early hours of the morning, before the Zen monks chant with their mala on the high ledges of Butan, and before men and women in the monasteries of the West take out their breviaries and Psalters, the contemplative prays alone, in humility, uniting himself with the One through meditative dialogue. Thomas Merton speaks of contemplative prayer as the prayer of the heart, where the contemplative through practice seeks God whether He answers or not. Here there is little of the formulaic; the expression is simple and may contain no words at all. Joy is not the goal of prayer and there are no guarantees that meditation will result in gifts from God. The contemplative is willing to enter into solitary prayer, aware that nothing earth-shattering may happen, that there may be no ecstasy, aware that the desert of the spirit is as valuable as the Joy. God disciplines His beloved, warning him against pursuing the gifts of the spirit for themselves alone. Thus the contemplative learns detachment in the empty chambers of this soul so that every spontaneous gift from the One is all the more beautiful because it is unexpected. Just as the Buddha learned under the Bodi tree that a tide of armed enemies is the same as the touch of a friend, for those who submit to the Love of God, it is in nothing that there is everything. All is the One.

Like the hero who leapt into a chasm that opened in the Roman forum, willingly responding to a divine call, the contemplative dives into the cleft of darkness, denying the illusion of cosmic duality. He rushes into the unknown, heedless of the risks, with his heart open, his spirit alive, understanding that he must move beyond the desert to the freedom of the mystical garden. Therefore, the contemplative fights the darkness with his heart, conquering fear with Love. He knows what men of the world do not, that all human constructs, even churches and temples, make barriers between God and his creation, supporting the false argument that man and God are separate. Through prayer and meditation, through practice and sacrifice, the contemplative follows a path until he sees that the darkness is in truth light in the union of opposites.

In meditation the mind is still. The solitary conversation is silenced, and the practitioner is open to the One. Established methods proven for thousands of years work best: sitting in zazen, repeating a mantra or the name of God, focusing on the flow of physical breath or the chakras, reflecting on a passage of religious writing, are sound ways to enter the One using this technique. The contemplative who wanders off on his own in meditation can often get into trouble. Thus, a well-grounded teacher or spiritual director is essential. Listening to God is both difficult and wondrous.

A contemplative, like the tree planted near running water, yields fruit in due season. It may take many years to reach a place where joy and suffering are One, where the path once obscured in spiritual youth is finally clear.

CALLING

When my parents and one of my daughters died within a six-month period, I was disconsolate. They had each succumbed to a painful disease, suffering a great deal before their deaths. One day, as I lay on my bed, wishing to die myself, I heard a voice saying, "Let me in." I saw the heavy curtains at the window begin to move. This was not the fatherly voice I had always imagined as coming from God, but a serious demanding presence. Again I heard it, "Let me in!" "No," I countered, shaking with terror. Then the curtains began flapping against the windowpane, and the papers I had been writing, full of self-pity, flew about the room. "Fine," I said in a resigned voice. "Come in then." The moment the words left my mouth, a charge raced through my body, leaving me for some reason calm and at peace. For the first time since my losses, I relaxed and slept deeply. When I awoke the next morning, the feeling of well-being continued. Finally, I believed I would recover. After that there were still terrible challenges, but I knew God was in control. I yelled at Him sometimes, but I was grateful for His care and trusted in His wisdom.

The contemplative must follow his path, the one that feels right to him, even if this goes against logic and even veers from reason. Unlike becoming a lawyer or an accountant, the development of the contemplative spirit is largely a matter of following the heart and listening to God's call. The danger here is that the individual may be lured by some romantic notion of what the contemplative life is truly like, instead of the discipline of prayer and the loneliness. Those who are caught up with the idea of prayer rather than prayer itself will probably not flourish in a monastery and will finally give up and move on to some other wonderful idea if they live in the world. One thing is certain: God's call is clear. All the contemplative needs is the courage to answer. For a long time I regretted not entering a cloister after college. I looked upon my decision to lead a normal life as a great mistake. Now I see that God had been using me all along to help those sent to me to know Him. He has tested my devotion in this earthly vineyard and humbled me with His fiery sword.

Cloud of Unknowing, cover me with your mantle of dread, that I may not stumble in my willfulness. May dread be my comforter and my consolation, so that I may cling closer to you.

Embrace me in your fearful wings, so that I might live in fear.

In the dark night past understanding, give me nothing so I may think nothing, do nothing, realize nothing and be nothing.

For when I am truly nothing, humbled past all experience, you may come and find me and purify my nothingness.

Shelter me from the storms of the ego and from the whirlwinds of desire.

Keep me safe from my enemy self who glows with pride and basks in my puny honors.

Deny me everything that I may want only You.

ADVISEMENTS

G od readies those He has chosen for a life of service. When the contemplative attaches himself to people and possessions, those things are sometimes removed. Often God does for the contemplative what he cannot do for himself. When there is pain and suffering, the individual is simply not ready to accede to Divine will. God is, however, ever generous, offering the gift of His Grace to those that He has elected to share the bounty of His love. The Grace of God is the shield of courage, the armor of hope, the sword of love. Grace brings with it relief and ultimately joy.

I have tried my vocation as a contemplative in the world. Attacked by dread, buffeted by fear and anxiety, my Love has finally matured. Many times I have lost my way altogether. But through death and destruction, with the help of God, I have prevailed. Although I have doubted God's wisdom, His love, even His presence, I have never doubted the insistent call to prayer and sacrifice that drew me first out of myself to the needs of others and then to surrender and God Himself.

It is vital to move away from petty concerns, which may seem insignificant and harmless, but which are in truth the seeds of the contemplative's destruction. Small annoyances, minuscule flashes of anger, glimpses of vitriolic reflection are the means by which the spirit attacks itself and wedges a gap between itself and the Beloved. Thus many well-meaning men and women systematically ruin their own happiness and block their spiritual progress, so immersed are they in the useless and inappropriate criticism of others. When the contemplative takes his eyes from God, everything goes awry. Ego and right thinking take over and humility flies away. Prayer and meditation are the cures for this disease and the malaise that is its symptom.

Like a climber on slippery rock, the contemplative often clings to his mundane life, grasping at family, loved ones and career, which are not truly real and will never belong to him despite his efforts to hold on too tightly to ephemeral things. Each day becomes a struggle or a flight from reality. He uses his will for his own purposes, building a church to his own ego, creating liturgy and ritual in his own honor. Reason becomes his God and denial his creed. Willpower is his fortress, and he clings to his mountainous path as though every action depended on his own ability to marshal his will into heroic action. He strives to develop self-esteem, make his own way, increase his self-confidence. He tries to create a circle of support and effective relationships as talk shows advise. He surfs the internet hoping some answer can be mailed to him from Amazon.com. He watches others achieve happiness and even contentment, and he wonders what on earth can be wrong with him when he is trying so hard. The fact is that nothing on earth is wrong with him.

Sometimes God is offered a consolation prize. The contemplative gives time to others, offering aid where it is needed. He does much more than his share, often denying himself pleasures to help those he encounters to be people of faith. He may become admired and develop a following of those he has mentored. This life of action may, for a time, convince him that he is doing enough, that he is living his life in accordance with God's will. When he sees those he has guided accept God and the path of faith, he will receive thanks from God, who loves him. The contemplative cannot shortchange God, only himself. When he says no to God's call to prayer, he is really saying no to himself and the joy he has been missing.

I have spent many days in bed hiding from what I needed to do. I even told people I was "hiding" when they asked about my whereabouts. This was my first response, when I understood the call to the contemplative life. I told myself I was too young, too busy, too lively and, of course, too intelligent to follow such a course. I remember reading *The Seven Storey Mountain* my sophomore year in college. My friends all read the book as well and deemed it insightful and important. That fall, during an enforced retreat complete with cold suppers, I read the book again, envying Merton and his courage and berating my own weaknesses. Therefore, I ran for my life from who I was, no matter how many signs God placed on the path before me. I developed brilliant arguments, formulated plans for the future, and pretended that I was happy. I took shelter in my intellect and concentrated on improving myself. However, each time I felt that old tug on my spirit, each time I headed back to my source, I felt greater joy at my return, as though I had in some ineffable way come Home. As Sappho has written, "and be four times blessed for all the hours of our separation."

Contemplatives are not without weakness. God bestows these as gifts in disguise to keep the contemplative from pride, ensuring that his ego will not overwhelm him. The more he sees his faults, the closer he comes to those first disciples who followed the Lord even unto death, dragging their impediments with them. St. Peter, with his passion and frailty, offers much hope to me. Christ often chose those with weaknesses to be closest to Him. A member of a religious community has a superior to guide him, but a contemplative in the world relies on a daily examination of conscience and, of course, aided by the criticism he receives. Unlike the monk or nun, the lay contemplative does not often have the opportunity to escape earthly temptations. So if he is honest with himself, he fortunately has some errors to correct. This protects the contemplative from the goody-two-shoes mentality that halts spiritual growth.

The contemplative life is hidden. Like those in the past who physically turned away form the crowd, the contemplative in the modern world keeps his relationship with God secret, first because few will understand it, and second because it is private and intimate. God has called the contemplative to His own secret garden, where He showers the beloved with the flowers of virtue, sensually girding him to be his envoy, holding him in His heady embrace. It is here in this hidden relationship that the contemplative momentarily grasps the notion of the Trinity, contemporaneously meeting the One as Father, Son and Spirit. This is another gift of the contemplative life, where experience greatly outweighs difficulties.

In monasteries prayer marks the rhythm of the nights and days. Those who live within the walls live a liturgical year, connected to the gospels and the psalms, moving in their spirit, growing in their grace. Those outside must make their way to a church, facing traffic, weather, and busy schedules to share common prayer. The rhythm of the day is broken by the world and its demands. Yet there is a sweetness to the hours stolen for God, because they have been obtained at such a cost. Each reading, psalm and prayer said with others brings with it many blessings because every moment is valued, every prayer is consecrated by the sacrifice made to share it with others. So too I make my own time for silent prayer, before I begin my classes, at the end of the day, when I am finally safely home in my driveway. I link my spirit to those who pray on far off hillsides, and lonely deserts, bringing myself into the contemplative community that stretches beyond individual churches and the vast abyss.

There is another darkness, which brings the contemplative to the precipice of despair. Even after many years of sincere practice and sacrifice, the contemplative may suffer what John of the Cross calls the dark night of the soul. In this horrible place the contemplative is riddled with bullets of doubt, fearful that his life means nothing, that everything he has relinquished has been foolish, and most of all, that God had abandoned him. In the wasteland of the spirit, where the grass blows away and the leaves are dust, the contemplative thirsts and waits for the One, even when he does not feel that his faith is stronger than fear. He continues to trust in the One, ever mindful of those who have given him examples, who are his guides in the darkness. I remember wondering why Jesus wept in the Garden of Gethsemane, begging his father to save him from crucifixion and death. It seemed illogical to me that Jesus would try to escape the task the Father had put before him. Only after I had been stripped of my former life did I truly understand the tears of my brother and Savior, who taught me how to suffer.

MEDITATIONS

Meditation rises out of life. When I was about eight, I went to confession on what used to be called Spy Wednesday, the day Judas made his bargain with the Romans. As I entered the church, I saw men I recognized from mowing the lawns working inside. They were bent over what appeared to be a huge piece of wood, hammering diligently near the marble font that contained holy water. As I moved closer, I felt a cold chill go through my body, because the men were nailing the image of Jesus to a great cross. "He was just coming loose, honey," the man said. Well, first I ran out the door as fast as I could. I kept seeing that terrible image before my eyes, even when I squeezed them really tight, and even when I hid my head under my pillow later. That mental picture, of everyday people nailing Christ to the cross, has been a great source of meditation over the years. What was so frightening to me as a child has brought me closer to Jesus, who was killed by men who mowed their lawns and thought they were doing the right thing, men who must have made mundane what was truly horrific.

One day, as I walked in the building where I worked, I saw a mallard duck on the sidewalk. It approached me and quacked appealingly. I greeted the duck with what I thought was a kind "hello." He seemed satisfied and headed to the person behind me. However, when the duck quacked this time he received no greeting. In fact, my colleague seemed embarrassed either for the duck or herself, and even beat me to the door. The duck tried again and again to be noticed, but students and teachers alike merely turned their heads at the little duck's attempts at communication. I realized that this is the way it is with God. No matter how many times He tries to reach His children, to express His Love, people busily hurry on, unmindful of His efforts. So too the contemplative may ignore His determined calls, expecting perhaps skywriting airplanes or talking ducks.

As a child I longed for my First Communion, even though the nuns told us a story about a little girl who died from joy when she first tasted the Holy bread. We marched to the front, the boys in the lines beside us scrubbed and chastened. The nuns' story had terrorized me at the time, but before I went to the altar rail my heart was beating wildly in my chest. I was filled with Joy. Oddly I do not remember actually receiving communion that morning. Later, my aunt gave me sterling silver rosary beads in a tiny circular case, and I felt a child's joy at being the center of attention. It was only in the weeks following that I felt what I perceived to be a force pulling me forward, toward something wonderful. Members of my class began to make less frequent trips to the sacrament, but my love for communion intensified as time went on. I became a regular.

I always remind myself that, in truth, I know nothing that although I have some knowledge of the Latin language, the Pre-Socratic Philosophers, and even the work of Thomas Merton, I only see bits and pieces of the universal mystery available to me, the information I have been able, with my limited ability, to acquire. Like the blind men with an elephant my estimations are probably both right and wrong. That does not matter. I am only a beginner in adding to my small storehouse of knowledge, something I have diligently been working on for many years. That is as it should be. The contemplative learns that a beginner's mind is essential to an intimate knowledge of God. To a beginner all things are new. Both everything and nothing are valid expectations. The joy is in the first effort.

As a new teacher, just out of my teens, I read a wonderful paper written by one of my sophomore boys. Perhaps because I was so inexperienced, I was amazed not only by the excellent verbiage but the care the student took to develop each idea and form each letter in every word he wrote. I remember being brought to tears that someone would apply so much effort to an assignment. I had written long comments on all the other papers, suggesting more precise words, variance in sentence type and length and attention to organization. However, when it came to this emblematic paper, I had nothing to say. So on an impulse I wrote just that: "What more is there to say? A." I often remember that diligent student, who, like a disciple of Christ, did so perfectly what he was asked to do. I pray that I may give my heart perfectly to my Lord without reservation, so that there will be nothing left to say.

A few days before my daughter died she painted beautiful watercolors of mushrooms, one of her favorite subjects. (We had mushroom rugs and ceramic work everywhere.) The last afternoon she was able to walk about, I helped her hang little mushroom paintings on the doors of several patients' rooms. This was her farewell gift to them. I wanted to have one for myself, or steal them all to keep forever, but I honored her wishes. I have thought of this often. God gives gifts to us just as Mari did, out of generosity and love. There is no why. Mari taught me to love others without reservation, the way that God loves me, and to accept gifts of the spirit without a question.

PETITIONS AND PRAYERS

God is selfish, teaching how unhealthy it is to be dependent on anyone other than Him. When human relationships flounder, it is often because one person is too dependent on another, looks to that person for happiness and fulfillment. With that sort of dependence, grief and desperation follow. Marriages fail, friendships dissolve, and whole families fall apart. God wants each dependent person, each person who becomes the source of life for others, to fall upon His mercy. He has created man to know Him, filled all with His infinite possibilities. He has even lived among His creatures, modeling a life of dependence on the Father, the Lord and Giver of Life. Yet often mankind fails to understand this simple point, that men are weak and flawed and cannot carry each other forever, that God alone can protect us from the storm.

I cast myself before You O Divine Father. Give me courage to live a life of faithfulness and to lean my mind and heart only on You.

Thomas Merton has written that "You are made in the image of what you desire." Thus the contemplative is not made in the image of what the active world approves, but rather in the image which he desires in the deepest part of his soul. Unfortunately society has placed a list of acceptable goals over his, superimposing pictures of busy active people and their accomplishments over his empty billboard. Therefore a contemplative grows up believing that there is something decidedly wrong with him, and that he should try to be like everyone else, piling up achievements that everyone can see and understand. Unfortunately, the satisfaction received is short-lived, because the contemplative is only truly happy when he is with God. He may wish for more because he is greedy and foolish, wanting everything active people have plus what God has given, but he soon learns that this is not possible. Occasionally, the contemplative in the world may find a partner to share his life, who also feels that God must come first in all things, sharing his desire to know God above all else. More often, however, the contemplative meets God in silence and solitude, conquering first the fear of loneliness and next loneliness itself. It is then that he realizes the image God had in mind for him from the beginning and joyfully becomes one with the image of His desire.

Only God has loved me completely. Although I have enjoyed human interaction, made many friends, I have always been a solitary. When I am alone, God speaks to me in my spiritual reading, talks to me in the dark and shows Himself to me in silence. He takes me into Himself, until I am no more.

Lord, let me be consoled by You and sheltered by You. Touch me with Your healing hands and hold me in the gentle shadow of Your arms. Let me find solace at Your spring of everlasting love.

After his death, Christ met with His friends and gave them His peace. He reminded them that He was in them, and that He had both given them the example of the ideal life and a list of instructions on how to live it. Therefore when the Sanhedrin ordered the followers of Jesus to stop preaching about Him, they refused to obey, speaking about Christ in the temples and anywhere they chose. They acted on faith, not fear. They knew that Jesus was in them, and so they were risking nothing by their actions. There are therefore no risks to a new endeavor for if we are in tune with God, He will not lead us astray. If we have given Him our ego, He will strengthen us. If we hold His word sacred, we will have the confidence to go forward.

Lord, you are in me, guiding me. Let me not take back my will and defeat myself. Let me dwell in Your peace instead, so that though I lose the illusion of power of my own actions, I live without anxiety in the whisper of Your gentle Love.

The Eucharist is the heart of my life. Whether it is flat disks imprinted with the design of a lamb, the sweet efforts of a first communion class or the heady loaves prepared by my brothers at the Weston Priory, I am most joyful when I receive the bread of Christ. Then I feel on my tongue the common food that connects me to countless Christians and all who believe in God's presence in our lives. As the bread melts away I experience the fuel of love spread through my heart, filling my chest, radiating through my limbs, awaking my appreciation of God made manifest in my physical body. As God provided bread to the Israelites in the wilderness, lest they starve on their journey, so too He fills me with the bounty of divine nourishment.

Thank you Lord Jesus for becoming bread in the desert of my solitude. May I never wish for more.

"The Lord is kind and merciful." I am reminded by the challenges of my life that everything that happens is good. Sometimes this is difficult to see, especially when I observe or experience suffering and death. Now I see that my daughter's death was a great mercy, because from it I learned to live in the moment, not the past or future. The chasm that existed for many years between me and my surviving daughter was a kindness, for it forced me to recognize and verbalize how miserably I failed her as a parent so that we could begin to love each other again. These lessons take time, requiring heavy doses of reality and maturity before understanding is clear. All of us want to think we are good people, that we are admirable in some way. It is not pleasant to examine our character defects or admit them to others. Yet this is necessary if we are to put pain in perspective and come to see it as an example of God's kindness and mercy.

When I am waiting I pretend that I am waiting for Jesus, that He is on His way and will be with me when He can. Then I don't mind if I wait a long time. I just think that He had probably met some people to help on the way and has just been delayed. St. Peter teaches that waiting should be an attentive action, not something that is merely an opportunity for sleep. The night He was betrayed, Christ asked His chosen ones to wait for Him when He went into the garden to pray. Instead, Peter, with James and John, forgot His instructions. So when waiting seems to be a chance for me to lose patience, I think that my Lord is nearby, ready when He comes from His duties. As I wait for Him to enter my heart in the course of the day, my beloved waits for me at the end of the path, ready to take me in His arms at the end of my final journey. He is the master of patience, teaching me how to live every day so that I may die with Him.

When my colleagues annoy me, I think of Christ's disciples, who in the gospels sometimes whine, reach foolish conclusions and ask a stream of stupid questions. This reminds me of my own thick-headedness. I have often laughed out loud when Peter wants to build tents on the mountain or believes that the Son of God can't feed a multitude. Part of my laughter is obviously directed at myself and my own inability to solve problems. How, then, can I not have compassion for my fellow workers who have me, not someone like Jesus, to contend with? The fact that Christ chose everyday people to spread His word is a dual lesson, that we should reflect on our own faults when confronted with the faults of others, that we should be thankful for God's abiding love in spite of our own short comings.

Call me Lord to my center. Remind me that life on the periphery of Your love will only bring fear and disassociation. You must continually call me, for sometimes I see a bird or flower or child or even a face ravaged by suffering and forget that is You. More than that, I forget that my own pain and disap-

pointments link me to Your humanity. However, when I am centered, not distracted by mundane affairs, I am not confused. All things rise and fall, come into being and fade away. A single red ant crossing cement soon disappears, leaving no trace behind. The center is nowhere and I am no one, disappearing into Your cloud.

For those who have forsaken us
And cast our love to the winds
Lord, hear our prayer

For those who assail us
And disturb our peace
Lord, hear our prayer

For those who rebuke us
With lies and deceits
Lord, hear our prayer

From those who feast
On the marrow of our bones
Oh Lord, protest us

From the armies of demons
Ready to destroy us
Oh Lord, deliver us

From the hidden enemies
And all the unseen faces of evil
Oh Lord, save us

For we are Your faithful ones
Marked by You from the beginning
Waiting patiently for the firestorm of years
And the second resurrection.

Oh Lord of Innocence
Have mercy on the children of Suffering
Have mercy on their sacred wounds
Have mercy on their ruined veins
Why have You scourged them
At the pillar of disease?
Virgin agony in Your garden
Of earthly delights
Such is Your treacherous Love
Lord have mercy
Lord have mercy
Lord have mercy

Lord grant me acceptance:
Of the path You have placed before me
Let me not falter as I reach for You
Christ hear me
Of those who rend my trust asunder
Let me put my faith in You alone
Christ graciously hear me
Of my limited understanding of Your will
Let me remember that You are infinite wisdom
Holy Redeemer hear me
Of the bitter fruit of life's experience
Son of God hear me
Of my own inflated ego
Let me know that You alone are God
Lord of Lords hear me

Give me the grade to seek holiness above all else
Even in the thorns around Your sacred heart
Where I must lay my head

Lord, let me love others
The way that You love me
Fully without reservation
For my self-satisfied smiles
Or the legions of sentences
That begin with I
Lord, let me love others
The way You love me
Freely without limitations
For the praise of intellect
Money or social position
That weaken the soul
Lord, let me love others
The way that You love me
Or cast me into utter darkness
Until I learn what You are teaching

Lord, open my ears that I might hear
The depth of Your silence
Open Your eyes that I might see
Beyond color and form
Open my mind that I might know
The emptiness of knowledge
Open my heart that I might receive
The peace of Your sacred heart
But do not open my lips, Lord
Until You have drenched my senses
In the refreshing river of Your love
And I am fit to speak Your word.

"Deliver me Lord from all anxiety"
Save me from briarwood of thought
That separates me from You
And the joy of Your promises
Grant me the grace to overcome fear
And feel the healing cross
You trace upon my brow
When I am heavy burdened.

Grant me O Lord a companion
To live with me in this life
And lead me to the next
Someone who like me
Knows the humming of Your universe
Who has seen the luminosity
Of Your gently Holy face
Who has heard the God of thunder
Who has felt the God of fire
If it be Your Holy will
Have mercy on my loneliness
The path is full of nettles
And it is hard to find my way

Just as it takes time to be accomplished in any field of active life, the contemplative must develop his talent for prayer and meditation, learning to bring concentration and dedicated practice to every aspect of his spiritual life. Although the first fruits of the contemplative life are sweet, they are not as satisfying as those harvested after years of labor. This is not a glamorous life where the practitioner lives only to be some kind of super-person, borne up by God when he wishes. Instead it is a life of daily work, daily bread and small harvests.

LCG

Giving away balloons on "Cider Days" Mount Holly, Vermont 2021

<u>About the Author</u>

Lynn Cronin Simek Geer was a Latin teacher, a writer, and a mother. A Magistra who shaped the lives of all those around her. She grew up in a small town in Upstate New York. Her Irish Catholic parents took her to catechism classes and First Communion at St. Patrick's Church. She graduated from Johnstown High School then attended The College of St. Rose where she majored in Philosophy and English Literature. Drawn toward a life of spirituality, she initially thought she would become a Carmelite nun.

One of her college courses required a semester of student teaching. She didn't want to do it, but it was a requirement. Through that course, she discovered that she loved teaching and she loved working with teenagers. She had always wanted a "house in the country," so after graduation, she married a boy from high school, and they moved into a restored pre-Revolutionary War house filled with period antiques. Her husband often entertained business clients at home, and Lynn learned to prepare gourmet cuisine by watching Julia Child. She taught high school English and Latin, but preferred teaching Latin. From the beginning, her teaching wasn't confined to the classroom. She filmed Super 8 movies with her students, and she wrote and directed plays for them.

Lynn had twin daughters. One was born perfectly happy and healthy. The other, Mari, was born deaf and was diagnosed with a rare blood disease. Her life expectancy was 12 years. Flying in her husband's private plane, they repeatedly took Mari to New York City for treatments, with many days and long hours spent in the hospital. Mari was strong willed and had periods of relatively good health. Lynn tried to give her a normal life. She drove the girls to private schools in Albany. There they had picnics and birthday parties, and vacations to Alaska and the Caribbean. Mari was enrolled in the Clarke School for the Deaf where she made lots of friends, played field hockey, and became a cheerleader.

Lynn continued her work in education, teaching Humanities and Latin at a small private school. She prepared Saturnalia feasts of suckling pigs, chaperoned student trips to Italy, and produced educational films for the American Classical League. She advised students in the classroom and outside of school, and she would often find lost teenaged souls, bring them home, and make them peanut butter and jelly sandwiches.

In 1983, Mari died at 16 years old. Shortly after, Lynn's mother died. A few months later, her father died. Lynn spent long days in the hospital with each of them, watching their lives fade away. In the space of six months, Lynn lost her daughter, her mother, and her father. Her husband filed for divorce soon after.

Lynn sunk into depression and alcoholism. She lived in a basement apartment in the city of Albany, conveniently located across the street from a liquor store. Her dark days became dismal. When men came to pick up her furniture to be reupholstered and she had no memory of ordering the work, she knew she needed help. She was in detox for 48 hours and regularly attended AA meetings from then on. She drove to Vermont to participate in spiritual retreats with the Benedictine Brothers of the Weston Priory. Newly sober, she again considered entering a convent but then decided to head to the Southwest to seek thought and prayer in the desert. She called a mover and found it cost too much to go to New Mexico. The farthest she could get with the money she had was North Carolina, so she went to Greensboro.

Because her New York teaching credits wouldn't transfer, she took required courses at UNC Greensboro. She got a job teaching Latin at three middle schools in the City of Highpoint as she worked toward her master's degree at Wake Forest University. Her teacher's salary couldn't make ends meet, so she got a part-time job at American Express selling credit cards over the phone. They soon made her a supervisor, and she began conducting training sessions. She started travelling to speak at conferences. Her boss came to rely on her to proofread his reports and critique his presentations, so when he was transferred to New York, he asked Lynn to come with him. With the new position, she would make double her teacher's salary and she could live in New

York. As much as Lynn would have liked the money and living in the city, she didn't want to leave teaching. She said no.

With her teaching certificate and her master's degree, she applied to high schools around Greensboro. At every interview, she insisted on meeting the football coach. Lynn had been a football fan since she'd learned the game while sitting on her father's knee, and she didn't want to work at a school that didn't have a good football team. Western Guilford High School had a good team, a great coach, and a wonderful principal who became a dear friend. There, Lynn found a new home.

Lynn's first classroom was a trailer out in the parking lot. She held "paideia" in her little Latin kingdom while the school underwent a renovation. When the addition was finished, Lynn had her choice of classrooms. She took the bright, sunny one at the end of the hall that looked out on the courtyard. She decorated it with artwork and posters, including a life-size cutout of Russell Crowe in *The Gladiator*.

In her new classroom, she performed her "Five Shows Daily." Students learned verb conjugations and made mosaics from tiny, cut-up pieces of paper. They learned noun declensions and how to march like Roman soldiers. They glazed pottery, picked grapes at a local winery, made wooden bowls on a lathe, and raced chariots around the school track. Her classes consistently scored high on the National Latin Exam. Every year, she sought out new students, specifically those in danger of falling through the cracks. She read through school transcripts, looked at IQ scores, and the bright, hopeful faces in 3rd grade pictures, and then made the kids take Latin. Lynn received the Coca-Cola Joseph B. Whitehead Award in 2002 and was the Guilford County Schools High School Teacher of the Year in 2004. But of equal importance to her was being allowed to stand on the sidelines with the coaches to cheer on the football team. Because if she was in the stands, parents would talk to her and she couldn't watch the game.

At Western, Lynn saw that the school's SAT test scores were below state average. She wanted to change that. She took dozens of practice tests, analyzed the SAT, and invented a program based on 12 simple rules. She called it "The 12 Things." Scores went up. Soon, there were too many kids to help after school, so they were invited to her house. She started a college counseling service and hired math and science tutors. She called the business "Via Vitae," the Path of Life.

In 2001, Lynn heard a voice tell her: "Call Tom Geer." She hadn't spoken to Tom in over 20 years. A friend convinced her to call him up. Using skills acquired as a teenager working the switchboard at Bell Telephone, Lynn tracked him down. They talked on the phone, and two months later they were married.

Lynn retired from the classroom and moved to Vermont to be near the Weston Priory. She and Tom bought a cottage in a little town with a village green and a general store. Her daughter, a class action lawyer, and her family stayed an important part of Lynn's life. And she never stopped tutoring; she never stopped mentoring. She taught test prep on Skype, helped draft college essays on Google Docs, and counseled students with phone calls and messaging.

With a text from the hospital in September 2023, she said goodbye to her last student.

Lynn's life was devoted to her students.
This book is for those she had not yet met.

Tom Geer Belmont, Vermont
April 2025

**Teaching on Market Street, Johnstown,
New York, 1944**

www.ingramcontent.com/pod-product-compliance
Lightning Source LLC
Chambersburg PA
CBHW020919140626
46545CB00015B/938